D0104301

Don't miss these other record-breaking books!

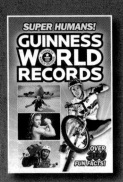

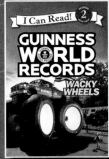

GUINNESS WORLD RECORDS

AMAZING BODY RECORDS!

by CHRISTA ROBERTS

HARPER
An Imprint of HarperCollins Publishers

Guinness World Records: Amazing Body Records!
© 2016 Guinness World Records Limited
The words GUINNESS WORLD RECORDS and related logos are
trademarks of Guinness World Records Limited.
All records and information accurate as of September 1, 2015.

Library of Congress Control Number: 2015952440
ISBN 978-0-06-234175-4

Design by Victor Joseph Ochoa
15 16 17 18 19   PC/RRDC   10 9 8 7 6 5 4 3 2 1
❖
First Edition

Guinness World Records holders are truly amazing, but all attempts
to set or break records are performed under controlled conditions
and at the participant's own risk. Please seek out the appropriate
guidance before you attempt any record-breaking activities.

TABLE OF CONTENTS

INTRODUCTION

Anyone, anywhere, has the potential to be a record-breaker! For over 60 years, Guinness World Records (GWR) has timed, weighed, measured, verified, and documented thousands of achievements in every category that you can imagine. There are over 40,000 current records!

Record-breaking is free to do. If the GWR adjudicators (the official judges who confirm records) approve your idea for a new record—or if you can prove you've bettered an existing title—you're on your way to becoming Officially Amazing!

Amazing Body Records! is the ultimate book about the ultimate machine: the human body. You'll meet people like Supatra "Nat" Sasuphan, the world's hairiest teen; Lucky Diamond Rich, the most-tattooed man (he gets new tattoos on top of the old ones!); the planet's loudest screamer and burper (yikes); and over 90 more amazing people whose unique talents and physical attributes have earned them a Guinness World Records title.

And who knows what you and your body can do! Maybe one day people will be reading about a new world record holder: **YOU!**

From braids to buzz cuts, blow-dries to crazy color combos, we put our hair to the test every day. But these record holders have taken their tresses, locks, and curls to totally new lengths and heights. Get ready to meet the hairiest family in the world, see a Mohawk spike that can touch the ceiling, and get the scoop about hair so strong it can pull a city bus!

THE 'FRO

American **Aevin Jude Dugas** has a big head of hair! It's no surprise that she won an Afro competition sponsored by a hair-care website. That's when Aevin's hair became the **largest Afro (female)** on record since March 31, 2012, measuring a fantastic 6.3 inches in height, 8.27 inches in width, and 4 feet, 7 inches in circumference. Aevin has been growing her hair for around 12 years. While she believes straight hair is beautiful, she decided that the pain and process of relaxing her hair wasn't something she wanted to go through. Photographs of her mother with an Afro also made her excited at the prospect of having equally large hair!

SPIKE IT UP

When **Kazuhiro Watanabe** of Japan walks through a doorway, he has to duck his head. It's not because he's unusually tall—it's his hair that reaches the sky! His hair was measured as the **tallest Mohawk spike** on October 28, 2011. When Kazuhiro's long locks are styled in his trademark do, it measures a full four feet high, which is larger than the height of an average five-year-old boy. For another comparison, think of your favorite slice of pizza—five slices would equal the length of his hair! Kazuhiro is a designer in Japan, and he loves collecting vintage American clothing. He's wanted to be a Guinness World Records holder for 20 years and it took six years to achieve this amazing goal!

Eric Hahn's hair also reaches new heights. He set the record for the **tallest full Mohican** at 27 inches high on November 14, 2008.

IRON MAN

Known as the Iron Man of Leicester, **Manjit Singh** is also known as something else: a multi–world record holder. His first record was set in 1987 for bench-pressing a weight of 56 pounds 1,035 times in one hour—but he wasn't content to stop there.

On November 11, 2009, Manjit pulled a double-decker bus almost 70 feet with his hair in Battersea Park, London, UK—the **farthest distance to pull a bus with hair**.

Manjit holds several records, all of which involve stamina. He says he enjoys setting records not only because they give him a sense of personal achievement, but because he has raised a lot of money for charity. In fact, he has raised thousands of dollars for worthy causes over the years.

ULTIMATE FACT:
Manjit had a "rocky road" to victory. Back in India, where he grew up, he lifted stones in his spare time!

HAIRY CHAMP

Karl-Heinz Hille from Germany is a superstar in the world of competitive beards and has competed in the Imperial Partial Beard category from 1999 to 2011. The guidelines stipulate that beards be grown on the cheeks and upper lip, and that the ends point upward and not curl over. Looks like Karl-Heinz is an expert at following the rules: he's earned the **most wins at the World Beard & Mustache Championships**, claiming the title eight times! The contest has taken place all over the world, from Sweden to Alaska. Karl-Heinz's most recent win took place in Norway in 2011.

NO SHAVING!

It's safe to say that **Sarwan Singh** hasn't had a close shave in quite some time. Instead, the Canadian looks after his superlong beard. Wouldn't you if you had the **longest beard**? It measured 8 feet, 2.5 inches when combed out to its full length on September 8, 2011. Watch where you step!

BEARDED LADY

As a little girl, it wasn't easy having whiskers. So American **Vivian Wheeler** began shaving when she was seven years old. But it didn't stop people from making fun of her. After four marriages and her mother's death in 1993, Vivian decided to stop trimming back her facial growth and let her beard grow. Now she's a mother of three and feels much happier with her life, having set the female record for the **longest beard** on April 8, 2011.

TOP 'STACHE

Did you ever think a mustache could be longer than your bed? **Ram Singh Chauhan** has one that is! This Indian man is the proud owner of the **longest mustache**.

Measured in Rome, Italy, on March 4, 2010, his mustache reached 14 feet!

PLAY (HAIR) BALL!

In December 2008, American barber **Henry Coffer** collected enough hair to make the **largest ball of human hair**—it weighed 167 pounds! Henry began saving the hair he clipped at the request of a customer. It took over 50 years to amass this giant hair ball! He's found many uses for his hair collection, including patching potholes, gardening, and fertilizing soil.

LONG LASHES

Some people might think that Floridian **Stuart Muller** has a hair in his eye. But that's not just any old hair. On December 7, 2007, he set the record for the world's **longest eyelash** with his record-breaking 2.75-inch-long eyelash growing away on his left upper lid. A normal eyelash, by comparison, is about 0.3 inches long.

NO PLUCKING REQUIRED!

Sumito Matsumura of Japan holds the record for the **longest eyebrow hair**, with his bushy brows clocking in at 7.1 inches on June 30, 2011. His eyebrow-raising record was announced on the Japanese television program *Nanikore Chin Hyakkei*. This beat the previous record, which stood at 7.01 inches, held by Sumito's fellow countryman Toshie Kawakami.

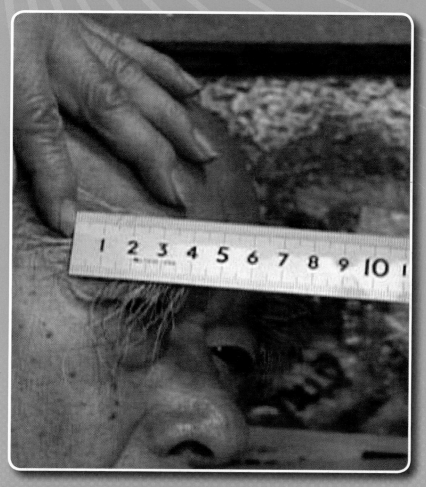

HAIRIEST TEEN

Supatra "Nat" Sasuphan from Thailand is like most teenage girls except for one thing: she set the record for **hairiest teenager** in 2010. Nat has hirsutism—excessive hair growth in women—but says it makes her feel special.

LARGEST HAIRY FAMILY

Larry, **Danny**, **Luisa**, and **Jesus Ramos Gomez** from Mexico are four members of a family of 19 that spans five generations. They all have a rare condition called congenital generalized hypertrichosis—in other words, they have a lot of hair! The women of this **largest hairy family** are covered with a light-to-medium coat of hair, while the men have thick hair on every inch of their bodies except their hands and feet.

Larry and Danny currently perform in the Mexican National Circus, and their success as acrobats has helped them deal with the prejudices they've faced. When the boys are not performing in the circus, they enjoy going out with their girlfriends and playing video games. Danny, the hairier of the brothers, says, "We have learned that people who are different can still have dignity."

LENGTHY LOCKS

Xie Qiuping of China stopped cutting her hair when she was 13 in 1973. That's why she has the world's **longest hair**: her remarkable locks measured a staggering 18 feet, 5.54 inches on May 8, 2004.

BRISK BRAIDS

And . . . go! **Aycan Kemal** from the UK completed a whole head of cornrow braids in a mere 15 minutes at the Afro Hair and Beauty Show held in London on May 29, 2011. She completed 26 braids in total, earning her the record of **fastest time to braid a person's hair**.

You could say that these record holders have really used their heads . . . and noses, ears, tongues, and teeth.

THE NOSE KNOWS

When people meet **Mehmet Ozyurek** from Turkey, they immediately see his world-record-holding body part: his nose. Mehmet has the **longest nose on a living person**. It measures 3.46 inches from the bridge to the tip and was verified on the set of *Lo Show dei Record* in Rome, Italy, on March 18, 2010.

FRUIT SMASH

This record holder takes the expression "hardheaded" to a whole new level. **Tafzi Ahmed** of Germany smashed more watermelons with his head than anyone in the world at the Rose Festival, in Saxony-Anhalt, Germany, on May 27, 2011. That day, he broke the record for the **most watermelons crushed with the head in one minute**. He was going for 50, but ended up crushing 43 in total. You might say it was a "smashing" success!

EAR POWER

Multiple record holder **Manjit Singh** not only has super-strong hair—he also achieved the **farthest distance to pull a single-decker bus with the ears**: 20 feet! He did this to raise money for the Manjit Fitness Academy in Loughborough, UK, on March 31, 2008. Now that's an earful!

SOCK-ET TO THEM!

Eyeing up yet another record on November 15, 2012, **Manjit Singh** raised the **heaviest weight lifted by both eye sockets**: 52 pounds, 14.5 ounces. He achieved the feat at Cossington Sports Hall in Leicester, UK, in celebration of Guinness World Records Day.

GUMMY MOMMY

Joyce Samuels from Los Angeles found a unique way to entertain her children when they were young. A gum-chewer since the age of 12, Joyce would place gum on her nose . . . and blow bubbles! That funny act has now earned her a world record. On November 10, 2010, this mom blew the **biggest bubble-gum bubble using the nose**, with a diameter of 11 inches, on the Los Angeles set of *Guinness World Records: Primetime.* Joyce chews the gum for at least an hour to get the sugar out before making it into a rectangle with her hands and putting it over her nostrils.

USE YOUR HEAD

How would you like to be taught by a world record holder? **Kevin Shelley** is an elementary school teacher from Indiana. He is a 20-year veteran of Tae Kwon Do and a fourth-degree black belt. As part of his martial arts workout, he has been breaking boards for a number of years. He has a special technique: he takes the boards and hits them over his head. Then, as one half of the board flies backward, he drops what is left in front of him. On July 30, 2008, in Mexico City, Mexico, Kevin smashed through 32 boards on the set of *El Show Olímpico*. He set a new record for the **most pine boards broken with the head in 30 seconds**.

PIGGY BANK REJECTS

Thomas Gartin from the UK holds the world record for the **most quarters held in the nose**. He held 14 quarters in his nose on the Los Angeles set of *Guinness World Records Gone Wild!* on June 29, 2012. The quarters had to be in the nose for 10 seconds without being assisted by hands.

HAMMER HEAD

John Ferraro of Massachusetts hammered 38 nails with his head, earning him the world record for **most nails hammered with the head in two minutes** in Milan, Italy, on June 19, 2014. John also holds the record for the **most nails hammered with the head in one minute** at 13. No surprise, his skull is three times the thickness of the average human's.

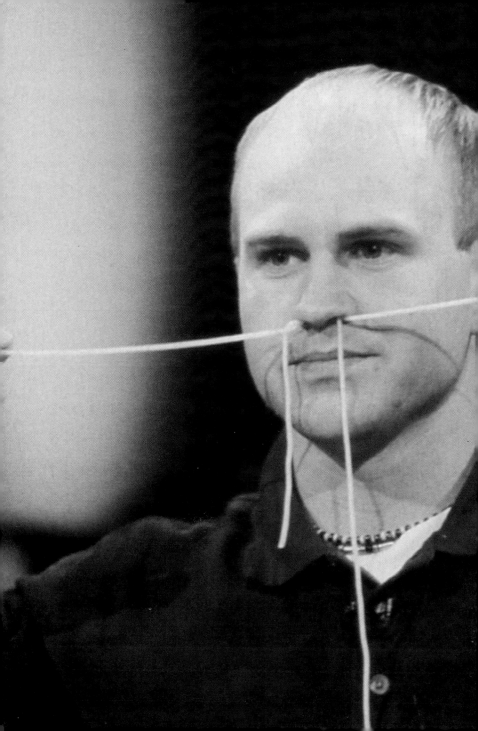

PROJECTILE PASTA

Sometimes record holders inspire each other. That was the case with **Kevin Cole** from Carlsbad, New Mexico. He always knew he had a large nasal cavity, and when he saw Matt Welsh set this record on TV, he believed that he might have the ability to better it. Kevin first started practicing his nasal ejection with ramen noodles and then progressed on to spaghetti. He set the record for the **longest spaghetti nasal ejection** in a single blow—7.5 inches—on the Los Angeles set of *Guinness World Records: Primetime* on December 16, 1998. Kevin has the ability to blow one end of the spaghetti out of one nostril and the other end out of the other nostril for a "nasal floss" effect.

NO STRINGS ATTACHED

If you give American **Justin Therrien** a string, he has a unique way of using it—he can make it travel through his body! Justin holds the record for the **longest string passed through the nose and pulled out of the mouth in one minute**. The string measured 255 feet, 2 inches when Justin performed the unusual act in Bellingham, Washington, on May 15, 2012.

EYES ON THE PRIZE

This record you truly have to see to believe. **Kim Goodman** from Chicago, Illinois, can boast the **farthest eyeball pop**! She can protrude her eyeballs a staggering 0.47 inches beyond her sockets. The eye-popping feat was measured in Istanbul, Turkey, on November 2, 2007. Kim discovered her talent when she was hit on the head, but can now pop out her eyes on cue. Measuring the "pop" is an exact science that has to be done by an optometrist using a device known as a proptometer. An average of three measurements gives the final, eye-watering result.

CHAPTER 3
Let's Talk About It

For some folks, opening their mouths is the first step to becoming a world record holder. In this chapter you'll meet the man with the biggest tongue, the person who painted the world's largest painting by mouth, and the baby born with the most teeth!

GUINNESS WORLD RECORDS

TONGUE WAGGING!

If American **Nick Stoeberl** sticks out his tongue at you, you can't miss it. That's because he holds the record for the **longest tongue**. His measures 3.97 inches from its tip to the top lip. Nick is a bank teller and a stand-up comedian. He has also been known to use his tongue—wrapped in plastic—to paint works of art!

BUBBLE GIRL

Pop! That's what happened to the former world record of nine bubbles when **Madison Julia Hill** blew 10 bubble-gum bubbles on June 8, 2014, in Ontario, Canada. That's the **most bubbles blown in one minute**!

LONG LICKER

Just a lick behind Nick, **Chanel Tapper** of the USA is the female record holder for the **longest tongue**. Hers measures 3.8 inches from the tip to the top lip. As a comparison, this is the same length as an iPhone 4. Chanel can eat a yogurt without a spoon, and get all of it out of the container using only her tongue!

TOTALLY LICKED

Say *ahhhh*! **Byron Schlenker** from New York holds the record for the **widest tongue**. His measured 3.37 inches at its broadest point on November 2, 2014. Byron previously held this record with a tongue width of 3.27 inches, but beat his own achievement!

BIG BITE

Brushing his teeth takes longer for **Vijay Kumar** from India than it does for most people. That's because he boasts the record for **most teeth**. He has 37, as counted on September 20, 2014. For context, the average adult has 32 gnashers.

BIG MOUTH

When **Francisco Domingo Joaquim "Chiquinho"** from Angola opens his mouth, viewers get an eyeful. He holds the record for the **widest unstretched mouth**. It was measured on the set of *Lo Show dei Record* in Rome, Italy, on March 18, 2010, at 6.69 inches. His mouth is big enough to fit a 12-ounce can of soda sideways.

HUMAN BOTTLE OPENER

If **Murali KC** from India can't locate a bottle opener, it's not a problem—he can use his incredible teeth. Murali holds the record for the **most bottle caps removed with the teeth in one minute**, taking off 68 caps at Country Club Mysore in Bangalore, India, on September 17, 2011.

METAL MOUTH

On the Los Angeles set of *Guinness World Records: Primetime*, on December 18, 1998, **Yim Byung Nam** of South Korea held a piece of metal the size of a silver dollar in his mouth for 14 seconds. That might not sound very impressive, but this wasn't just any metal: it was heated to 910 degrees Fahrenheit, the **hottest metal in the mouth**. Yim first heated the molten metal in a small pot, where the temperature reading was taken. The metal was then poured onto a brass spatula before being placed into his mouth. Yim spat it out on a plate after he was through and incredibly it was still hot enough to fry bacon. A sizzling performance!

CHEW ON THIS!

Some people are born to become record-breakers, and some claim records the very day they are born. On April 10, 1990, **Sean Keaney** was born in the UK with 12 teeth, setting a world record for the **most teeth at birth**. His teeth had to be removed to prevent possible feeding issues, but that was no problem for Sean—he grew his second full set at 18 months.

TEAM EFFORT

Seventeen feet high and 70 feet long is the size of the **largest painting by mouth (by a team)**! It was created by **Tesco Dukes Green** in Feltham, Middlesex, UK, on August 17, 2013.

ULTIMATE FACT:
Tooth enamel is the hardest substance in the human body—harder even than bone.

MOUTH MASTERPIECE

The **largest painting by mouth by an individual** is *Mother Teresa Service to the World*. This artwork is 30 feet long and 20 feet high and was painted by **R.Rajendran** of India. It was presented and measured on October 30, 2007, and commemorates Mother Teresa's work with the poor.

DON'T FORGET TO BRUSH!

Some people have strong arms. Other people have strong legs. **Frank Simon** of the USA has strong . . . teeth! He first achieved the **greatest weight balanced on teeth** by holding a motorbike with his gnashers in 1998. He has since bettered his record on several occasions, the last time supporting a 140-pound refrigerator for 10 seconds on the set of *Circo Massimo Show* in Rome, Italy, on May 17, 2007.

You've got to hand it to these amazing people: their hands and nails have earned them a spot in the record books. From the woman with the longest fingernails ever to the living person with the most fingers and toes, everyone in this chapter deserves a round of applause.

BUFF AND POLISH

Whether driving, bathing, doing the chores, or even cutting her grandchildren's hair, there wasn't much **Lee Redmond** of the USA couldn't do with her nails. Pretty amazing considering that they were the **longest fingernails ever for a woman** at over 28 feet combined! Lee began growing her nails in 1979 and has said it was to get attention after growing up in a large family. Lee's nails were the result of her careful weekly nail maintenance, which involved soaking them in warm olive oil and taking 48 hours to paint them. Lee was offered $10,000 to cut her nails off but chose to keep them, enjoying showing off her unique hands to children and teaching them that it's okay to be different. Sadly, Lee lost her fingernails in a car crash in 2009.

NAIL ROYALTY

Amazing doesn't even scratch the surface of these talons! American **Chris "The Dutchess" Walton** holds the female record for the **longest combined fingernails on both hands**. They measure in at 11 feet, 10 inches for her left hand and 12 feet, 1 inch for her right hand, totaling 23 feet, 11 inches, as confirmed on September 16, 2013. The total length of her fingernails is as tall as an average male giraffe! The Dutchess is a rock singer and recording artist. She has been growing her nails for 18 years.

NAILING IT

When **Melvin Boothe** of the USA had his fingernails measured in Troy, Michigan, on May 30, 2009, they had a combined length of 32 feet, 3.8 inches—making him the record holder of the **longest fingernails ever**.

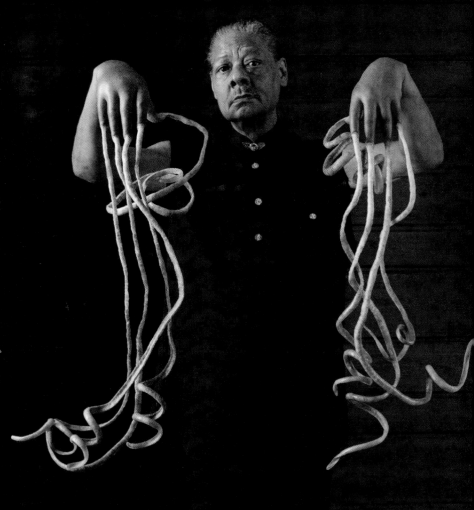

PLAY BALL!

You might say **Muhamed Kahrimanovic** of Germany is hands-on. He holds the record for the **most baseball bats broken with his hands in one minute**—55! He did this at Mo San sports center in Hamburg, Germany, on November 17, 2010, in celebration of Guinness World Records Day.

DOUBLE DIGITS

Indian **Devendra Suthar** has a total of 28 digits—the **most fingers and toes on a living person**, resulting from a condition known as polydactylism. Devendra's 14 fingers and 14 toes were verified in Himatnagar, Gujarat, India, on November 11, 2014.

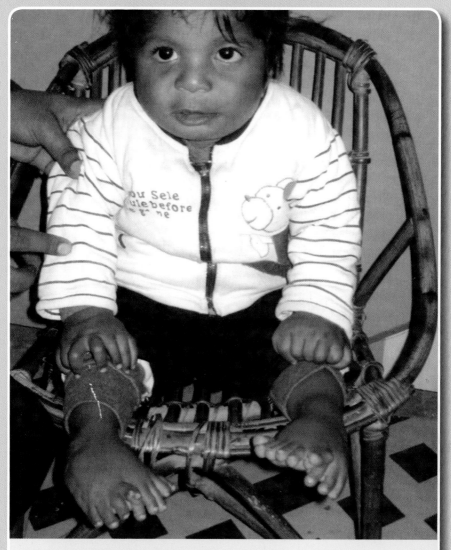

The **most fingers and toes at birth** are 14 fingers (7 on each hand) and 20 toes (10 on each foot) and belonged to **Akshat Saxena** of India, born in March 2010. Akshat has had an operation and now has the standard number of digits on both hands and feet.

ALL HANDS ON DECK

Sarah Chapman from the UK has hands made for walking! She covered a distance of a whopping 16,404 feet on her hands at Glastonbury, Somerset, UK, on June 3, 2002, achieving a record for **farthest distance walking on hands in eight hours**.

If you ever thought pinkie fingers couldn't be strong, think again! **Kristian Holm** of Norway holds the record for the **heaviest weight lifted with little fingers**, raising 148 pounds, 12 ounces on November 13, 2008. And one record wasn't enough for this "heavy-weight"—he also set the record for the **single little finger deadlift** (pictured) on the same day.

CHAPTER 5
Total Body

Whether it's a world record because of age or endurance, or a posterior that can play video games, these records all achieved by the human body are totally, humanly awesome!

SISTER BOND

On August 2, 1999, **Kin Narita** and **Gin Kanie** became the **oldest female twins ever**. These twin sisters had a bond unlike any other. Kin and Gin (their names mean "Gold" and "Silver" in Japanese) were born in Nagoya, Japan, on August 1, 1892. Their lives spanned three centuries and they witnessed the Japanese eras of Meiji, Taisho, Showa, and the current Heisei. Both enjoyed good health and each had big families, with 16 children, 15 grandchildren, 16 great-grandchildren, and one great-great-grandchild between them. Although Kin died of heart failure in 2000 at the age of 107, and Gin a year later, they are still household names in Japan, having appeared regularly on TV and in commercials.

BROTHERS FOR LIFE

The **oldest male twins ever** authenticated were **Glen** and **Dale Moyer** of Ohio, on March 28, 2000, in the USA. The pair, named after valleys (a glen and a dale), were born into a farming family on June 20, 1895.

The brothers were so close growing up that they both chose their birthday as their wedding day. Dale, a farmer, was married to his wife, Mary, for 75 years. Glen, a teacher, celebrated his 78th anniversary with his wife, Mabel, in 1999.

Glen passed away on April 16, 2001, at the age of 105 years, 9 months, 26 days; Dale celebrated four more birthdays, passing away in July 2004. The twins had said of their long lives, "We are just pleased to have lived this long and to be as happy and as comfortable as we are."

A LIFE WELL LIVED

Born in France on February 21, 1875, **Jeanne Louise Calment** lived to the ripe old age of 122 years, 164 days, the greatest fully authenticated age to which any human has ever lived. She set the record for the **oldest person ever**. Jeanne was only 14 when the Eiffel Tower was completed in 1889. She led an extremely active life, taking up fencing at 85 years old and still riding a bicycle at 100. Jeanne played herself at the age of 114 in the film *Vincent and Me*, becoming the **oldest actress** in a film. She became a star attraction in Arles, where she met Vincent van Gogh in 1888. Her humor was sharp right up until her death. Her customary reply to visitors who said "Good-bye and until next year, perhaps?" would be "I don't see why not! You don't look so bad to me." This special lady, who former French President Jacques Chirac once said was a bit of a grandmother to everyone in France, died at her nursing home in Arles, France, on August 4, 1997.

SUPER SKIN

No stretch of the imagination needed here, just some stretchy skin! On October 29, 1999, **Garry Turner** from the UK achieved the record for the **stretchiest skin**. He is able to stretch the skin of his stomach to a whopping 6.25 inches due to a rare medical condition called Ehlers-Danlos syndrome, a disorder of the connective tissues affecting the skin, ligaments, and internal organs. With this condition, the collagen that strengthens the skin and determines its elasticity becomes defective, resulting in, among other things, a loosening of the skin and hypermobility of the joints.

ULTIMATE FACT:

Hula-Hoops caught on as a fad in the USA in the 1950s, but hoops had been used for fun and exercise for many years before that. In ancient Greece, boys exercised with a bronze ring called a trochus.

HUNG UP ON HOOPING

Pippa "The Ripper" Coram of Australia set the record for the **most fire hoops spun while doing the splits**. On September 14, 2012, Pippa spun three burning Hula-Hoops around her arms and neck for 10 seconds while performing the splits. The hoops are specially created for the act, with wicks attached around the outer perimeter.

Fellow Australian **Kareena Oates** hooped it up on June 4, 2005. She spun 41 Hula-Hoops around her waist, sustaining three full revolutions between her shoulders and her hips on the set of *Guinness World Records* in Sydney, Australia. She earned her world record for **most Hula-Hoops spun while suspended from the wrists**.

LIVING DOLL

You might say that **Cindy Jackson** is hooked on cosmetic surgery. Since 1988, this American woman has spent $99,600 on 47 cosmetic procedures, including nine full-scale surgical operations, earning her the record for **most cosmetic procedures** on February 7, 2005. These have included three full face-lifts; two nose operations; two eye lifts; liposuction of the knees, waist, abdomen, thighs, and jawline; lip and cheek implants; chemical peels; chin-bone reduction; and semipermanent makeup.

Cindy grew up in an agricultural community in a small Midwestern town. After studying art in college, Cindy moved to London, UK, and when she received a small inheritance in 1988, her lifelong affinity for cosmetic surgery began. Ever the art connoisseur, Cindy based her look on Leonardo da Vinci's theory of a classically proportioned face. Dubbed "the human Barbie doll," Cindy dedicates herself full-time to cosmetic surgery research, frequently speaking at medical conferences and to women's groups. She also models occasionally and writes regular features for several British publications.

NO STOPPING HER

Do you think you could shimmy for three hours? **Melanie White** proved she's got the moves! This Australian dancer holds the record for the **longest belly dance shimmy**, clocking a duration of 3 hours, 7 seconds at the Live Life Expo in Moruya, Australia, on February 25, 2012. Melanie's goal was to promote belly dancing as a performance art of great physical and cultural depth.

MARATHON WOMAN

Margaret Hagerty of the USA didn't let her advancing age stop her from doing new things. She began running at age 66 and has since completed 73 marathons. Her record attempt began on November 5, 1995, at the age of 72, and finished on July 4, 2004, when she was 81 years, 101 days, making her the **oldest woman to complete a marathon on each continent**.

MARATHON MAN

After he lost his brother John to cancer in 1999, **Robert Rebello** set a series of challenges for himself. The American became the **oldest man to complete a marathon on each continent**, running his final marathon in Antarctica on February 28, 2011, at 74 years, 281 days. His efforts have seen him raise thousands of dollars for kidney cancer research in memory of his sibling.

DAREDEVIL

Lights, camera, action! The **longest career as a stuntman** is currently held by Brit **Rocky Taylor**, who started his professional career in 1961. Rocky's father, Larry Taylor, was a stuntman and actor, which is how Rocky got into the stunt world. He prepares for each role very carefully, and safety is his primary concern. In his entire career, he's been injured only 14 times, but he was never worried about getting back up and preparing for the next role. He was last seen on screen in Brad Pitt's 2013 zombie movie *World War Z*.

NO BUTTS ABOUT IT

Butt seriously. Originally described by publisher Ubisoft as "the first video game you can play with your butt," *Rayman Raving Rabbids TV Party*, which was released in Europe on November 18, 2008, is the **first game controlled by the posterior**! The "Beestie Boarding" mini game is controlled by sitting on the Wii Balance Board and shifting one's weight from cheek to cheek.

A NOT-SO-TYPICAL WORKDAY

On January 29, 1972, **Vesna Vulovic** of Serbia had a very lucky escape. The former air hostess was on board a DC-9 plane when it blew up midair flying over Srbsk in Czechoslovakia (now Czech Republic). Despite plummeting from 33,333 feet up, incredibly she wasn't killed, having fallen inside a section of tail unit. Vesna was in the hospital for 16 months, but her determination to pull through means she can now lay claim to the **highest fall survived without a parachute**.

MEDICAL MARVEL

Adam Rainer, an Austrian who lived from 1899 to 1950, measured 3 feet, 10.5 inches at the age of 21. He then suddenly started growing at a rapid rate and by 1931, he had reached 7 feet, 1.83 inches. He became so weak as a result of this incredible growth spurt that he was bedridden for the rest of his life. At the time of his death on March 4, 1950, Adam measured 7 feet, 8 inches, and held the record for **most variable stature**. Adam was the only person in medical history to have been both a dwarf *and* a giant.

MOST ALBINO SIBLINGS

Of the eight children born to Americans George and Minnie Sesler, the four eldest of their five sons (three of whom are pictured) were all born with the rare genetic condition albinism. Identical twins **John** and **George**, and **Kermit** and **Kenneth Sesler**, who have all since passed away, were all born with translucent skin, pinkish-blue eyes, and white hair.

Sharing this record, the four children of Americans Mario and Angie Gaulin—**Sarah**, **Christopher**, **Joshua**, and **Brendan Gaulin**—all born in the 1980s, were born with the rare genetic condition oculocutaneous albinism. Their father also has the condition and their mother carries the gene.

The Sesler brothers and Gaulin siblings hold the record for **most albino siblings**.

CHAPTER 6
Feet First

Step aside and let these record holders take the stage with their fancy footwork! From the woman with the longest toenails to the world's toe-wrestling champions to the biggest feet on the planet, take a walk through some of the most outrageous world records around!

WALKING ON EGGSHELLS

On June 5, 2012, things were looking sunny-side up for serial record-breaker **Ashrita Furman** of the USA. That's the day he achieved the record for the **most eggs crushed with the toes in one minute**! Ashrita demolished 55 eggs in New York City that day. And what's even more eggstraordinary? His feet were tied together—and that's no yolk!

Ashrita has held many Guinness World Records titles, including this one. He's even held the title for the **most Guinness World Records titles**! He set his first record in 1979. He has since set more than 500 records, many of which still stand.

BEST FOOT BACKWARD?

If **Moses Lanham** of Michigan wants to put his feet up, the question is, which way will they be facing? That's because Moses has a special ability to rotate his feet backward, achieving the record for the **largest foot rotation**—120 degrees—in Milan, Italy, on March 10, 2011. One record wasn't enough for the man known as Mr. Elastic. On the same day he also achieved the **fastest time to walk 20 meters** (65.6 feet) **with the feet facing backward**: 19.59 seconds! Moses feels no pain when he rotates his feet—in fact, he says that keeping his feet in a twisted position is actually more comfortable for him.

GOING TO GREAT LENGTHS

You won't find a pair of toenail clippers in **Louise Hollis**'s home. This California mother of 12 and grandmother of 21 has the world's **longest toenails**. Louise stopped cutting her toenails in 1982. She wanted her feet to look pretty in sandals for the summer. When her toenails were measured at their longest in 1991, the combined length was 87 inches. These titan toenails make wearing shoes difficult, so when she does, they must be open-toed and have at least three-inch soles to prevent her nails from scraping the ground.

ULTIMATE FACT:
Louise keeps all of her broken toenails.

QUEEN OF TOES

One toe-wrestling world championship wasn't enough for **Karen Davies** of the UK. She has been champion a *toe*-tal of four times in the women's category from 1999 to 2002, making her the **most successful female toe wrestler**. At the contest held in Wetton, UK, contestants had to push an opponent's foot to the other side of a specially constructed ring called a "toerack" using only their toes.

KING OF TOES

Going toe-to-toe with Karen Davies, **Alan "Nasty" Nash** of the UK is the **most successful male toe wrestler**, with six world championship titles to his name (1994, 1996–1997, 2000, 2002, and 2009). Competitors play with their bare feet as they attempt to pin their opponent's foot on a platform. The best out of three matches is declared the winner.

BIG FEET

If **Jeison Orlando Rodriguez Hernandez** from Venezuela walks into a shoe store, it's unlikely he'll find what he's looking for. He holds the record for the **largest feet**. His right foot measures 1 foot, 3.79 inches and his left foot 1 foot, 3.59 inches, as confirmed on October 6, 2014. Here, Hernandez, who stands 7 feet, 3 inches tall, is pictured with his nephew.

FANCY FOOTWORK

Gabriel Pereira Campanha of Brazil achieved the **fastest time to solve a Rubik's Cube using the feet**. He did it in 27.17 seconds in São Paulo, Brazil, on April 5–6, 2014.

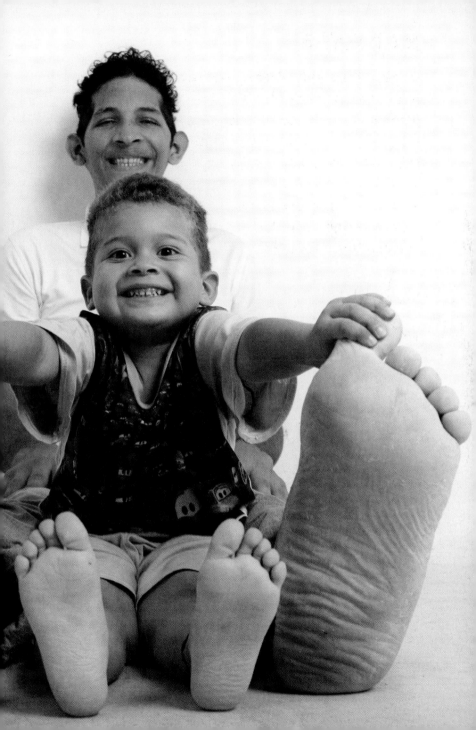

WHO'S HUNGRY?

If **Rob Williams** offers to make you a sandwich, you might be surprised how fast he makes it—with his feet! This Texan made a bologna, cheese, and lettuce sandwich in 1 minute, 57 seconds on November 10, 2000, in Los Angeles, California, achieving the record for the **fastest feet-made sandwich**. Rob had to take two slices of bread out of a loaf packet, remove the rind from a slice of bologna, take the plastic off slices of processed cheese, and add lettuce, sliced tomatoes, mustard, mayo, and sliced pickles. He then cut the sandwich in half and presented it on a plate. Rob didn't skimp on the presentation—he even added olives on cocktail sticks!

THE BIG SQUEEZE

The **most juice extracted from grapes by an individual in two minutes** is 5.36 gallons, and was achieved by **Martina Servaty** of Germany on the set of *Guinness World Records— Die größten Weltrekorde* in Cologne, Germany, on September 13, 2008.

EGGS-TREME

The **fastest time to put six eggs in egg cups using one's feet** is 27.42 seconds, achieved by Japanese actress **Miho Suzuki**. She attempted the record live on the set of *24 Hour Television: Love Saves the Earth* in Tokyo, Japan, on August 21, 2011.

SHARP SHOOTER

Nancy Siefker, an American circus performer, hit the mark in Los Angeles, California, on June 20, 2013. She fired the **farthest arrow shot into a target using the feet**, slinging it in from a distance of 20 feet. Even more impressive? The guidelines require a target of no more than 12 inches in diameter—but Nancy hit a target measuring just 5.5 inches.

TAKE A LOAD OFF!

On December 5, 2012, in Beijing, China, **Guo Shuyan** put his best feet forward and achieved the **heaviest weight balanced on the feet**! On the set of *CCTV Guinness World Records Special*, he balanced a large urn—filled with sand bags and one of the show's presenters—with his feet! All totaled he balanced a whopping 784 pounds, 13.6 ounces!

These people decided to change their bodies in the most amazing and wild ways. Their individual, fearless alterations to their skin, hair, tongues, and more have not only made them look like no one else, but have also earned them a place in the record books. Read on to meet some of the world's most colorful personalities.

EXPRESSING HERSELF

Maria Jose Cristerna, a mother of four in Mexico, holds the female record for the **most body modifications**. Known as the Mexican Vampire Lady, she has over 49, including tattoos; implants on her forehead, chest, and arms, including titanium "horns"; and multiple piercings in her eyebrows, lips, nose, tongue, earlobes, belly button, and nipples. Maria grew up in a very religious family, and says she always knew she was different. People in her neighborhood used to cross the street in fear when they saw her coming, but Maria doesn't want to hurt or scare anyone. She's just being who she wants to be.

NOT YOUR AVERAGE SENIOR

This British body-modder born in 1930 has said he wanted to stand out a bit in the crowd. And as the record holder for the **most-pierced senior citizen**, **John Lynch** does just that. A former bank manager, John got his first piercing on his eyebrow in his forties. And he's never looked back. He was counted as having 241 piercings, including 151 in his head and neck, in London, UK, on October 17, 2008.

A HUMAN WORK OF ART

Isobel Varley of the UK had tattoos all over her body, including her head! In fact, she was the **most-tattooed female senior citizen**. Isobel went to a tattoo convention when she was in her late forties and became hooked. On April 25, 2009, tattoos covered 93 percent of her body as revealed on the set of *Lo Show dei Record* in Milan, Italy. Sadly, she passed away in May 2015.

A LEPPARD NEVER CHANGES HIS SPOTS . . .

Tom Leppard of the UK is Isobel Varley's male counterpart as the **most-tattooed senior citizen**. Known as the Leopard Man of Skye, Tom is an ex–special forces soldier who joined the Royal Navy when he was only 15, and was sent to Africa, where he lived for over 30 years. About 99.9 percent of his body is covered with a leopard-skin design, with all the skin between the dark spots tattooed saffron yellow.

NOT AFRAID OF NEEDLES

Elaine Davidson (Brazil/UK) received her first skin piercing in 1997, and had been pierced a staggering 4,225 times as of June 8, 2006—the **most piercings in a lifetime**. The former restaurant owner is constantly adding and replacing jewelry, mostly in her face. She enhances her exotic looks with tattoos and bright makeup, and often wears feathers and streamers in her hair.

When Elaine was examined on May 4, 2000, she had a total of 462 piercings—making her the **most-pierced woman**. This included 192 piercings on her facial area, including ears, forehead, eyebrows, chin, and nose, and 30 on her tongue alone. But it doesn't stop there! She also had 56 piercings on her body, including her stomach, breasts, and hands.

FACE FIRST

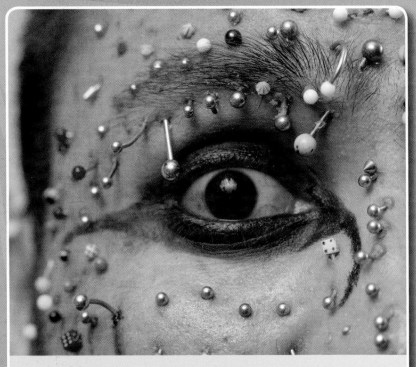

With 280 facial piercings, **Axel Rosales** from Villa Maria, Argentina, holds the distinction of having the **most face piercings** as of February 17, 2012. The initial count was 271, but Axel wanted a more rounded number for his record, and so he asked a friend who was a piercer to add nine more to take it up to 280!

BITE YOUR TONGUE

When New Jersey resident **Francesco Vacca** sticks out his tongue, it's a mouthful! He boasts 16 piercings, which was the **most piercings in the tongue** as of February 17, 2012.

LIVING IN FULL COLOR

For the ultimate in full-body multilayered tattooing, look no further than Australian performance artist **Lucky Diamond Rich**, the **most-tattooed man**. Lucky has spent over 1,000 hours having his body modified by hundreds of tattoo artists and has a full collection of colorful designs from around the world sketched over his entire body. But not content with stopping there, Lucky decided to go for a 100 percent covering of black ink, including on his eyelids, the delicate skin between his toes, down into the ears, and even his gums! He is now being tattooed with white designs on top of the black, and colored designs on top of the white!

When he isn't getting tattoos, Lucky can be found riding his unicycle, swallowing swords, and juggling chain saws.

I THEE MODIFY?

The couple that stays together . . . body modifies together. That's how it is with **Victor** and **Gabriela Peralta**, who wed on February 21, 2008, and became the **most-body-modified married couple**. Victor, a native of Uruguay, and Gabriela, from Argentina, share a total of 84 modifications: 50 piercings, 8 microdermals, 14 body implants, 5 dental implants, 4 ear expanders, 2 ear bolts, and 1 forked tongue. Victor and Gabriela, who also are both covered with tattoos, say they don't care what people might think about all their modifications—they love their body art and each other!

LOOKING SHARP

No stranger to needles, the world's **most-pierced man** is **Rolf Buchholz** from Dortmund, Germany. On August 5, 2010, Rolf had 16 piercings in his right ear, 15 in his left ear, 25 in his eyebrows, 8 in his nose, 94 in and around his lips, 2 in his tongue, 3 in his nipples, 4 in his navel, and enough around the rest of his body to come in at 453 in total!

Another record held by Rolf Buchholz is the **most body modifications for a male**: 516. This was verified in Dortmund, Germany, on December 16, 2012. Rolf's body modifications include his hundreds of piercings, two subdermal "horn" implants, and five magnetic implants in the fingertips of his right hand, among others.

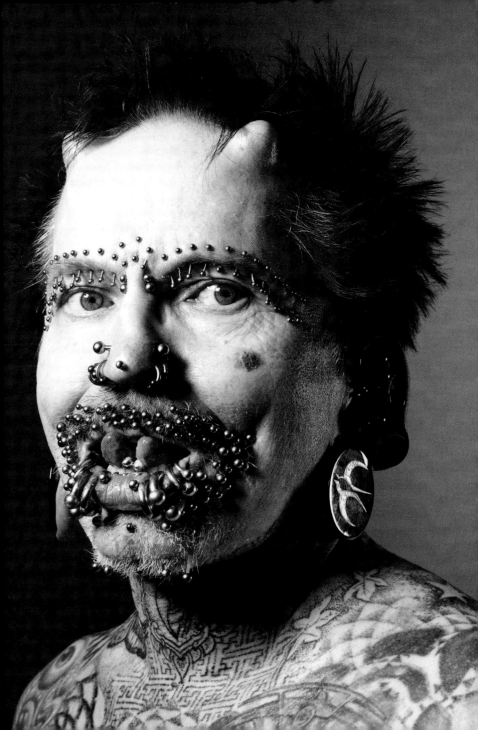

CHAPTER 8
It Takes All Sizes

When it comes to being a record holder, size does matter. Super small or extra tall, these folks have used their stature and weight to achieve some amazing records. You're about to meet the smallest man ever, the world's heaviest woman, *and* the tallest teenagers on the planet!

SHORTEST MAN

Chandra Bahadur Dangi of Nepal held the distinction of being the **shortest living man**. He measured 21.5 inches tall: about the size of six stacked cans of soup.

Chandra lived in the isolated Nepalese village of Reemkholi. He spent his days making place mats and head straps, and helped look after the village's buffalos and cows.

He was the seventh of eight children, and had five brothers and two sisters. He was looked after by his immediate older brother and his family. Three of his five brothers were less than four feet tall, while two sisters and two brothers are average height.

Chandra loved being a record holder and traveling all over the world to promote his country. Sadly, he passed away in September 2015, but he still holds on to the title of **shortest man ever**.

INCREDIBLE BULK

Italian **Daniele Seccarecci** had a healthy appetite. Good thing, because he was the **heaviest competitive bodybuilder** in the world. His competition weight was 297 pounds. The competition weight must be taken when the person is participating in an internationally recognized bodybuilding competition, and the body is therefore at its best form. Daniele normally weighed 300 pounds. Sadly, Daniele passed away in 2013.

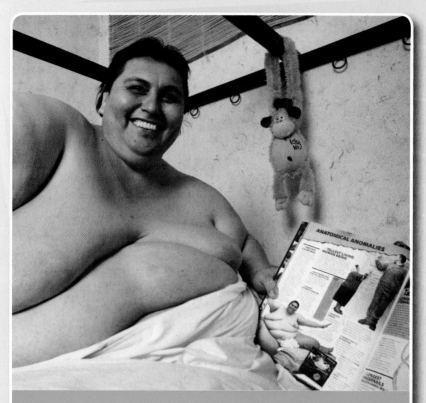

HEAVIEST MAN

In January 2006, **Manuel Uribe** from Mexico weighed in at 1,235 pounds, making him the **heaviest living man**. Manuel battled his weight for many years. After making a television appeal and with medical assistance, he did begin to have some success shedding the pounds. By December 2009, his weight stood at 917 pounds, but this crept up again to 980 pounds by March 2012. Sadly, Manuel passed away in 2014.

SHORTEST WOMAN

When **Jyoti Amge** from India turned 18, she celebrated by getting a world record! On December 16, 2011, her birthday, she was measured at the Wockhardt Superspeciality Hospital in Nagpur, India. And at 24.7 inches, she claimed the record for **shortest woman** from American Bridgette Jordan. Jyoti is no stranger to being a record holder. She had previously held the title for the **shortest female teenager**. Her small stature is due to a form of dwarfism, but her tiny size isn't stopping Jyoti from dreaming big. She hopes to be a Bollywood actress and model!

SPORTING HEAVYWEIGHT

You don't want to mess with **Sharran Alexander** of the UK. She's the **heaviest sportswoman**, weighing in at 448 pounds on December 15, 2011. Sharran actively competes all around the world as an amateur sumo wrestler and is recognized by the British Sumo Federation in the UK.

Sharran says her size is an advantage and that she's never felt any pressure to gain or lose weight. Her advice to aspiring athletes? "Just follow your heart and do what you want to do."

HEAVIEST WOMAN

Pauline Potter from Sacramento, California, is the world's **heaviest woman**. She weighed 643 pounds on May 13, 2010.

Pauline believes that being over-weight is in her genes—her mom was over 400 pounds and her dad was over 600. She says that growing up, her family used food to celebrate and to comfort.

Pauline needs a scooter to get around and can no longer get into her car. Despite these limitations, Pauline is a positive person. She has many good friends and enjoys bingo, shopping, and scrapbooking. Pauline hopes that one day she might get another record—for the woman to lose the most weight.

BIG BABES

Mary Ann Haskin of Arkansas gave birth to the world's **heaviest twins** on February 20, 1924. Patricia Jane Haskin weighed 13 pounds, 12 ounces, and her brother John weighed 14 pounds. That's a total of 27 pounds, 12 ounces!

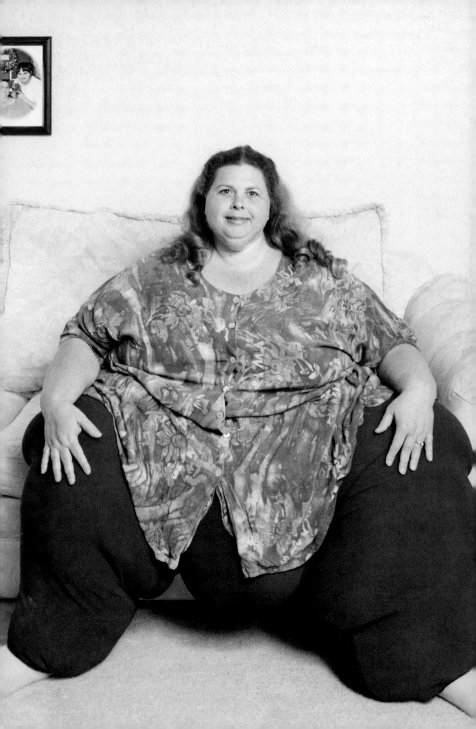

TALLEST MAN

How many times do you think **Sultan Kösen** gets asked if he plays basketball? Probably a lot, considering he's the **tallest man** in the world! Born in Turkey in 1982, Sultan measured 8 feet, 3 inches on February 8, 2011. He was the first man over eight feet to be measured by Guinness World Records in over 20 years.

Sultan also has the **largest hands** of any living person! They measure 11.22 inches from the wrist to the tip of the middle finger, and his hand span is 12 inches.

Sultan is one of five siblings, with three brothers and one sister. The rest of his family, including his mom and dad, are all average size.

LONGEST LEGS

Svetlana Pankratova of Russia holds the record for the world's **longest legs**. They measured 51.9 inches in Torremolinos, Spain, on July 8, 2003. Her record-breaking legs helped her in a basketball career at Virginia Commonwealth University in Richmond, Virginia, where she was a major player who set two school records, which are still unbroken.

THAT'S A CINCH!

An aficionado of Victorian-era clothes, **Cathie Jung** decided to start wearing a belt to gradually reduce her 26-inch waist so she could wear them. Since 1983, she's worn a corset 23 hours a day, only taking it off to shower. The result? She has the **smallest waist** in the world today. Her corseted waist measures 15 inches. Un-corseted it measures 21 inches. Cathie, a mother of three, refined her waist with the help of her husband, Bob, an orthopedic surgeon. She does not eat a special diet or exercise to maintain her figure. She says, "We had no intention of setting a record. It was about dressing appropriately for the age."

TALLEST MALE TEEN

If you're a kid, **Kevin Bradford** is the kind of person you want to have around when the cookies or candy are kept on the top shelf. On April 30, 2015, at 16 years, 185 days, the Florida teen measured 7 feet, 1 inch tall, making him the world's **tallest male teenager**.

The **tallest teenager ever**, meanwhile, was American **Robert Wadlow**, who stood 8 feet, 0.38 inches at the age of 18 in 1936.

TALLEST FEMALE TEEN

On March 19, 2014, **Rumeysa Gelgi** of Turkey was measured at 7 feet, 0.09 inches, officially becoming the **tallest female teenager**.

TALL TALES

This pair takes love to new heights—literally. The **tallest married couple** is **Sun Mingming** and his wife, **Xu Yan**, both from China. He measured 7 feet, 8.98 inches while she stood 6 feet, 1.74 inches, making a combined height of 13 feet, 10.72 inches when measured on November 14, 2013. They were married in Beijing, China, on August 4, 2013.

TALLEST BASKETBALL PLAYER

Sun Mingming also holds the record for the **tallest basketball player**. He plays for the Heilongjiang provincial men's basketball team! Not to be left on the sidelines, Xu Yan plays handball for the Heilongjiang provincial women's team!

TALLEST MAN EVER

The **tallest man ever** in medical history was American **Robert Wadlow**, who when last measured on June 27, 1940, stood a staggering 8 feet, 11.1 inches tall.

RACE TO THE FINISH

Running a marathon takes endurance, stamina, and training—and bodyguard **Charles Bungert** from Camarillo, California, has them all. Weighing 427 pounds, 9 ounces, Charles is the **heaviest person to complete a marathon**, finishing the Los Angeles Marathon on March 17, 2013. Bungert crossed the finishing line with a time of 8 hours, 23 minutes, 52 seconds. After the race, Bungert commented: "I'm not planning on going for another record." Though he did add that he might consider it if someone breaks his record.

After eight chapters of the ultimate stories of human achievement, you might be thinking there aren't any human body records left to break. Not so! After you read about these extraordinary people, you'll know that there's always another record to be achieved. Sometimes funny, sometimes wacky, these are records that can only be described as *outrageous*.

HE ATE WHAT?

Frenchman **Michel Lotito**, born in 1950 and known as Monsieur Mangetout (translation: Mr. Eats Everything!), began eating metal and glass at age nine. No wonder that he holds the record for **strangest diet**!

Gastroenterologists X-rayed his stomach and described his ability to consume two pounds of metal per day as unique. And that's an understatement! His diet included 18 bicycles, 15 shopping carts, 7 TV sets, 6 chandeliers, 2 beds, a pair of skis, a low-calorie Cessna light aircraft, and a computer! He is said to have provided the only example in history of a coffin (handles and all!) ending up inside a man.

Monsieur Mangetout first became aware of his strange skill when a glass from which he was drinking broke and he began chewing the fragments. By October 1997, he had eaten nearly nine tons of metal.

Mr. Lotito died of natural causes on June 25, 2007.

A NOT-SO-LADYLIKE SOUND

Burrrrrpppppp! That's the sound that earned **Elisa Cagnoni** of Italy her world record at the 13th Annual Hard Rock Beer Festival "Ruttosound" competition. In Reggiolo, Italy, on June 16, 2009, her **loudest burp (female)** was recorded at 107.0 decibels (dB)! The competition raises money for charity, and attracts about 30,000 people on the night when all the best burping champions compete!

AN EVEN BIGGER BURP!

Paul Hunn blasted out a burp at 109.9 dB on August 23, 2009, earning him the record for the **loudest burp** overall! Paul practices his talent by drinking a lot of fizzy drinks, and allowing the gas to build up in his stomach.

COVER YOUR EARS!

When her students get out of hand, **Jill Drake** from the UK knows how to get them to cover their ears. That's because Jill holds the record for the **loudest scream**—one that reached 129 dB when measured at the Millennium Dome in London, UK, in 2000. As a comparison, a police whistle is 80 dB, a lawn mower is 100 dB, and a thunderclap is 120 dB. Jill broke the record on her very first attempt—and believes she developed her vocal skills from working in the classroom!

BREAK IT DOWN

German break-dancer **Benedikt Mordstein** holds the record for **most consecutive elbow hops**! He reached 66 when he made the attempt in Germany on November 10, 2011, in celebration of Guinness World Records Day.

PEE-YEW!

How's this for a job? **Madeline Albrecht** was employed at the Hill Top Research Laboratories in Cincinnati, Ohio, a testing lab for products by Dr. Scholl. She worked there for 15 years and had to smell literally thousands of feet and armpits during her career. She has sniffed approximately 5,600 feet and an indeterminate number of armpits, achieving the record of the **most feet and armpits sniffed**!

GET IN A SPIN

Belgian Cirque de Soleil artist **Youssef El Toufali** didn't let dizziness get in the way of his record—even after 137 head spins! That's the **most head spins performed in one minute**.

GET TO THE POINT

Natasha Veruschka of the USA is known as the Queen of Swords. That's because, on September 3, 2004, she swallowed 13 swords at the Third Annual Sideshow Gathering and Sword Swallowers Convention, in Wilkes-Barre, Pennsylvania. That's the **most swords swallowed simultaneously by a female**! Each sword was at least 15 inches long. Natasha is also a belly dancer.

DOWN THE HATCH

Australian daredevil **Chayne Hultgren**, aka the Space Cowboy, set a cutting-edge record. On September 12, 2012, at the Guoman Hotel in London, UK, he swallowed 24 swords—the **most swords swallowed at once by a male**!

LONGEST-LIVED HUMAN CELLS

Henrietta Lacks, an American woman, died from cancer on October 4, 1951, at John Hopkins Hospital in Baltimore, Maryland. Cells from her cervical cancer were taken both before and after her death. Known as HeLa cells, they became the first human cells to survive and divide outside the human body, earning the achievement of **longest-lived human cells**.

The descendants of these tumor cells still survive and are used in medical research around the world in diverse areas including cancer research, polio vaccination, and in vitro fertilization. Millions of Henrietta's cells have been manufactured and have been referred to in more than 60,000 research papers.

Henrietta Lacks was buried in an unmarked grave to which a headstone was only added in 2010, donated by a doctor who had read a biography of Lacks.

SWEET SOUND!

Georgia Brown of Brazil had the **greatest vocal range** at eight octaves, extending from G2 to G10, as of August 18, 2004. The highest note that she hit, the G10, is technically not a musical note but a frequency. The full range was verified by music experts using a piano, violin, and Hammond organ.

A HAPPY B-ENDING

Super-flexible acrobat **Leilani Franco** (UK/Philippines) boasts the **fastest time to travel in a contortion roll**, traveling 65 feet, 7.2 inches in just 17.47 seconds at the Royal Festival Hall in London, UK, on March 11, 2013. A contortion roll requires contortionists to start with their feet on the ground before arching backward and propelling themselves forward in a chest-down roll.